DALE ALLMAN

Soothe Your Anxiety

How to Use Music and Sound on a Pathway to Calmness

Contents

Foreword

Anxiety and stress affect over 300 million people worldwide according to the World Health Organization. Let that number sink in for a minute.

There are many effective treatments and professional resources that only 25% of those affected take advantage of. What do the other 75% do? Suffer in silence? Talk to friends and family?

The latest scientific research and key findings point to a number of DIY or self-empowerment tools and practices that anyone can use. This book is the second of three, designed to provide practical advice and pathways to a calmer you.

Stay peaceful!

1

Introduction

The Importance of Addressing Anxiety and Stress

In today's fast-paced world, anxiety and stress have become ever-present elements of modern life. According to the World Health Organization, over 264 million people worldwide suffer from anxiety disorders, making it the most prevalent mental health condition globally. Stress, too, is an ever-present part of our daily lives, often stemming from work, relationships, financial pressures, and a myriad of other sources. The impacts of chronic stress and anxiety are profound, affecting not only mental health but also physical well-being. Elevated stress levels can lead to issues such as high blood pressure, cardiovascular disease, weakened immune function, and even increased mortality rates.

Traditional treatments for anxiety and stress, including psychotherapy, medication, and lifestyle changes, are effective but not always accessible or desirable for everyone. In this context, exploring alternative and complementary therapies becomes crucial. Among these, music and sound therapy emerge as powerful, non-invasive tools capable of enhancing well-being and reducing anxiety and stress.

Why Music and Sound?

Music and sound have been integral to human culture and healing practices for millennia. From the ancient Greeks, who used music to treat various ailments, to indigenous cultures worldwide, which have long understood the healing properties of sound, the therapeutic potential of music transcends time and geography. Modern science is now catching up, providing empirical evidence supporting what our ancestors instinctively knew: music and sound can profoundly impact our emotional and physical health.

This book aims to delve into the rich history and modern applications of music and sound, providing practical guidance on how you can harness these tools to outsmart your anxiety and stress effectively. Whether you are looking to supplement existing treatments or seeking alternative methods to improve your well-being, the healing power of sound offers a compelling, accessible option.

2

Understanding Anxiety and Stress

What Are Anxiety and Stress?

Anxiety and stress are terms we often hear in everyday conversations, yet their precise meanings and how they impact our lives can sometimes be misunderstood. This chapter aims to clarify these concepts and provide a foundation for understanding how music and sound can help manage them.

Anxiety: A Closer Look

Anxiety is a natural response to stress and can be beneficial in certain situations. It can alert us to danger, help us stay focused, and motivate us to solve problems. However, when anxiety becomes excessive or persistent, it can interfere with daily life and lead to more serious health issues.

Anxiety disorders are the most common mental health disorders, affecting millions of people worldwide. They encompass a range of conditions, including generalized anxiety disorder (GAD), panic disorder, social anxiety disorder, and specific phobias. Common symptoms of anxiety include:

- Persistent worrying or fear
- Restlessness or feeling on edge
- Rapid heart rate
- Shortness of breath
- Sweating
- Trembling
- Fatigue
- Difficulty concentrating

These symptoms can vary in intensity and duration, but they often result in significant distress and impairment in social, occupational, or other important areas of functioning.

Stress: The Body's Response to Pressure

Stress is the body's way of responding to any kind of demand or threat. When we sense danger—whether real or imagined—the body's defenses kick into high gear in a rapid, automatic process known as the "fight-or-flight" response. This response is the body's way of protecting itself.

When functioning properly, stress can help you stay focused, energetic, and alert. In emergency situations, stress can save your life, giving you extra strength to defend yourself. However, beyond a certain point, stress stops being helpful and starts causing major damage to your health, mood, productivity, relationships, and quality of life.

Common signs of stress include:

- Physical symptoms such as headaches, muscle tension, or digestive issues
- Emotional symptoms such as irritability, anxiety, or depression
- Behavioral symptoms such as changes in appetite, procrastination, or substance abuse

Chronic stress can lead to serious health problems, including heart disease, high blood pressure, diabetes, and other illnesses, as well as mental disorders like depression and anxiety.

The Science of Stress Response

Understanding the science behind how our bodies respond to stress can empower us to manage it more effectively. When you encounter a perceived threat, your hypothalamus—a tiny region at your brain's base—sets off an alarm system in your body. Through a combination of nerve and hormonal signals, this system prompts your adrenal glands, located atop your kidneys, to release a surge of hormones, including adrenaline and cortisol.

Adrenaline increases your heart rate, elevates your blood pressure, and boosts energy supplies. **Cortisol**, the primary stress hormone, increases sugars (glucose) in the bloodstream, enhances your brain's use of glucose, and increases the availability of substances that repair tissues. Cortisol also curbs functions that would be nonessential or detrimental in a fight-or-flight situation. It alters immune system responses and suppresses the digestive system, the reproductive system, and growth processes. This complex natural alarm system also communicates with the brain regions that control mood, motivation, and fear.

Once the perceived threat has passed, hormone levels return to normal. As adrenaline and cortisol levels drop, your heart rate and blood pressure return to baseline levels, and other systems resume their regular activities. However, when stressors are always present and you constantly feel under attack, this fight-or-flight reaction stays turned on. The long-term activation of the stress-response system—and the subsequent overexposure to cortisol and other stress hormones—can disrupt almost all your body's processes.

Common Triggers of Anxiety and Stress

Identifying what triggers anxiety and stress in your life is the first step towards managing them effectively. Triggers can be external or internal:

External Triggers

- **Work-Related Stress:** Deadlines, heavy workload, conflicts with colleagues, or job insecurity.
- **Relationships:** Conflicts with family members, friends, or partners.
- **Financial Issues:** Concerns about money, debt, or financial stability.
- **Life Changes:** Major changes such as moving, starting a new job, or going through a breakup.
- **Environmental Factors:** Noise, pollution, or living in a high-crime area.

Internal Triggers

- **Negative Thought Patterns:** Pessimistic outlook, excessive worry, or self-criticism.
- **Health Issues:** Chronic illness, pain, or fatigue.
- **Perfectionism:** Setting unrealistic expectations for oneself and feeling anxious when they are not met.
- **Lack of Control:** Feeling helpless or unable to change your circumstances.

Managing Anxiety and Stress: A Holistic Approach

Managing anxiety and stress involves addressing both the symptoms and the underlying causes. Traditional approaches include therapy, medication, and lifestyle changes such as exercise, healthy eating, and adequate sleep. While these methods are effective, integrating alternative therapies, such as music and sound, can provide additional relief and enhance overall well-being.

The Healing Power of Music and Sound

In the chapters that follow, we will explore how music and sound can be powerful tools in managing anxiety and stress. We will delve into the science of how sound affects the brain, discover different types of therapeutic sounds and music, and learn practical techniques for incorporating these tools into your daily life. Whether you are looking for a complement to traditional treatments or seeking a new path to wellness, the healing power of music and sound offers a compelling, accessible option.

By understanding anxiety and stress and how they impact our lives, we lay the groundwork for a journey into the world of music and sound therapy. Through this journey, we will discover how these ancient practices, supported by modern science, can help us find peace, relaxation, and a greater sense of well-being.

3

The Science of Music and Sound

Music and sound are more than just entertainment; they are powerful tools that can profoundly affect our minds and bodies. In this chapter, we will explore how sound interacts with the brain, the specific frequencies known for their healing properties, the scientific research supporting music therapy, and the unique benefits of bilateral music or sounds. Understanding these aspects will provide a solid foundation for utilizing music and sound to manage anxiety and stress.

How Sound Affects the Brain

When we listen to music, a complex and fascinating process unfolds in our brains. Sound waves enter our ears and are transformed into electrical signals that travel through the auditory pathway to various parts of the brain. This journey triggers a range of responses that can influence our emotions, thoughts, and physical state.

The Auditory System and Brain Pathways

Sound waves are captured by the outer ear and funneled through the ear canal to the eardrum. Vibrations from the eardrum are transferred to the three tiny bones in the middle ear (the malleus, incus, and stapes), which amplify the sound and send it to the cochlea in the inner ear. The cochlea, a spiral-shaped organ filled with fluid, contains thousands of hair cells that convert these vibrations into electrical signals.

These electrical signals travel along the auditory nerve to the brainstem, where they are processed and relayed to different brain regions, including the auditory cortex, which is responsible for interpreting sounds. The auditory cortex is part of the temporal lobe, an area crucial for processing sensory input and forming memories.

Neuroplasticity and Sound

One of the most remarkable aspects of the brain is its neuroplasticity, the ability to reorganize itself by forming new neural connections throughout life. Music and sound can stimulate this neuroplasticity, leading to long-term changes in brain structure and function.

Studies have shown that musicians, for instance, have increased gray matter in areas of the brain involved in auditory processing, motor control, and spatial coordination. Listening to music can also enhance neuroplasticity, helping to improve cognitive functions, emotional regulation, and resilience against stress.

The Healing Frequencies

Certain sound frequencies are believed to have specific healing properties, influencing the body and mind in unique ways. Three well-known concepts in this realm are the use of particular hertz (Hz) frequencies, binaural beats and bilateral music.

Specific Frequencies

- **432 Hz:** Often referred to as the "natural tuning" frequency, 432 Hz is said to resonate with the natural vibrations of the universe. Proponents believe it promotes relaxation, reduces anxiety, and brings a sense of harmony and balance.

- **528 Hz:** Known as the "love frequency" or "miracle tone," 528 Hz is associated with DNA repair, healing, and transformation. It is believed to have a profound impact on overall well-being.

Binaural Beats

Binaural beats are created by playing slightly different frequencies in each ear, leading the brain to perceive a third tone that is the mathematical difference between the two. This phenomenon can entrain the brain to specific states, promoting relaxation, focus, or sleep.

For example, if a 300 Hz tone is played in one ear and a 310 Hz tone in the other, the brain perceives a binaural beat of 10 Hz. Different binaural beats can target various brainwave states:

- **Delta (1-4 Hz):** Deep sleep and relaxation
- **Theta (4-8 Hz):** Meditation, creativity, and deep relaxation
- **Alpha (8-12 Hz):** Relaxed alertness and stress reduction
- **Beta (12-30 Hz):** Active thinking and focus

The Benefits of Bilateral Music and Sounds

Bilateral music or sounds involve alternating audio stimulation between the left and right ears. This technique is often used in therapies such as Eye Movement Desensitization and Reprocessing (EMDR) and has been found to be particularly effective in reducing anxiety and promoting relaxation.

How Bilateral Stimulation Works

Bilateral stimulation engages both hemispheres of the brain, encouraging communication and coordination between them. This can help to process and integrate emotional experiences, leading to a reduction in anxiety and stress. When listening to bilateral music, sounds or tones move rhythmically from one ear to the other, creating a soothing and balancing effect.

Research and Applications

1. **Anxiety Reduction:** Research has shown that bilateral stimulation can significantly reduce symptoms of anxiety. A study published in the *Journal of EMDR Practice and Research* found that participants who received bilateral auditory stimulation experienced a decrease in anxiety levels and an improvement in mood.
2. **Trauma Processing:** Bilateral sounds are often used in trauma therapy to help individuals process distressing memories and emotions. By facilitating the integration of traumatic experiences, bilateral stimulation can reduce the emotional intensity associated with these memories.
3. **Enhanced Relaxation:** Bilateral music can promote a state of deep relaxation, making it an effective tool for stress management. The rhythmic alternation of sounds helps to calm the nervous system and encourage a sense of balance and well-being.

Practical Tips for Using Bilateral Music

- **Headphones:** Use headphones to ensure that the audio alternates effectively between the left and right ears.
- **Ambient Settings:** Choose a quiet, comfortable environment to enhance the relaxing effects of bilateral music.
- **Duration:** Start with short sessions (10-15 minutes) and gradually increase the duration as you become more accustomed to the experience.
- **Guided Sessions:** Look for guided bilateral music sessions or apps that offer structured programs designed to reduce anxiety and promote relaxation.

Music Therapy Research

The field of music therapy has grown significantly in recent years, with numerous studies demonstrating its effectiveness in reducing anxiety, stress, and other mental health issues. Here, we explore some key findings and the practical applications of music therapy.

Overview of Scientific Studies

1. **Reduction of Anxiety and Stress:** Research has shown that listening to calming music can lower cortisol levels, reduce heart rate, and alleviate symptoms of anxiety. A study published in the Journal of Music Therapy found that participants who listened to music experienced significant reductions in anxiety compared to those who did not.

2. **Improvement in Mood:** Music can enhance mood by stimulating the release of dopamine, a neurotransmitter associated with pleasure and reward. A study in the journal *Nature Neuroscience* highlighted that listening to music activates brain regions involved in reward processing, similar to the effects of other pleasurable activities.

3. **Therapeutic Applications in PTSD:** Music therapy has been used effectively in treating post-traumatic stress disorder (PTSD). A study in the *Journal of Traumatic Stress* reported that music therapy sessions helped reduce PTSD symptoms and improve overall psychological well-being in veterans.

4. **Enhanced Cognitive Function:** Music training and listening have been linked to improved cognitive abilities, including better memory, attention, and problem-solving skills. A review in *Frontiers in Psychology* discussed how music enhances neuroplasticity, supporting cognitive development and resilience.

Case Studies and Testimonials

- **Hospitals and Clinics:** Music therapy is often used in medical settings to help patients manage pain, reduce anxiety before surgery, and enhance recovery. For example, a case study at a pediatric hospital found that children undergoing surgery experienced lower anxiety and faster recovery times when exposed to music therapy.

- **Mental Health Facilities:** In mental health care, music therapy helps individuals express emotions, improve communication, and build coping skills. Testimonials from patients in these settings frequently highlight the transformative impact of music therapy on their mental health journey.

Conclusion

The science of music and sound is a rich and fascinating field that bridges the gap between art and medicine. By understanding how sound interacts with the brain, recognizing the healing properties of specific frequencies, exploring the extensive research supporting music therapy, and appreciating the benefits of bilateral music or sounds, we can fully grasp the profound potential of music and sound in managing anxiety and stress.

As we move forward in this book, we will delve into practical applications and techniques, providing you with tools to incorporate music and sound into your daily life for enhanced well-being. Whether you are looking to complement traditional treatments or explore new pathways to health, the science of music and sound offers a promising and accessible approach.

4

Practical Applications

I n this chapter, we will explore practical ways to incorporate music and sound into your daily life to help manage anxiety and stress. From selecting the right music to engaging in therapeutic sound practices, these strategies can become valuable tools in your wellness toolkit.

Creating a Personalized Music Playlist

One of the simplest yet most effective ways to use music for anxiety and stress relief is to create personalized playlists. These playlists can be tailored to different moods, activities, and times of day.

Steps to Create a Playlist

1. **Identify Your Needs:** Determine what you want to achieve with your playlist. Are you looking to relax, boost your mood, or focus on a task?
2. **Select Music That Resonates:** Choose songs that evoke the desired emotional response. For relaxation, opt for slow-tempo, soothing tracks. For a mood boost, select upbeat, energetic songs.
3. **Mix It Up:** Include a variety of genres and artists to keep the playlist engaging. Sometimes, a mix of instrumental and lyrical pieces can enhance the experience.

4. **Test and Adjust:** Listen to your playlist and see how it affects your mood and stress levels. Make adjustments as needed to ensure it meets your goals.

Examples of Playlists

- **Relaxation Playlist:** Include tracks like classical music, ambient sounds, and soft jazz.
- **Mood Boosting Playlist:** Add upbeat pop, rock, or dance tracks that make you feel happy and energized.
- **Focus Playlist:** Incorporate instrumental music, such as piano, acoustic guitar, or electronic chill-out music, to aid concentration.

Integrating Music into Daily Routines

Incorporating music into your daily routines can make a significant difference in managing stress and anxiety. Here are some practical ways to do this:

Morning Routine

Start your day with calming music to set a positive tone. Play gentle, uplifting tunes while you get ready for the day. This can help reduce morning anxiety and create a sense of calm.

Work and Study

Listening to instrumental or ambient music while working or studying can improve focus and reduce stress. Avoid music with lyrics if it tends to distract you. Consider using binaural beats to enhance concentration and productivity.

Exercise

Create a high-energy playlist for workouts. Upbeat music can motivate you to exercise more intensely and make the experience more enjoyable. For activities like yoga or stretching, choose soothing music to help you stay relaxed and focused.

Evening Wind Down

Use music to transition from the busy day to a relaxed evening. Play soft, slow-tempo music during dinner or while winding down before bed. This can help signal to your body that it's time to relax and prepare for sleep.

Guided Meditation and Relaxation Sessions

Guided meditation and relaxation sessions that incorporate music or sound can be powerful tools for reducing anxiety and stress. These sessions often use specific sounds or music to enhance the meditative experience.

Types of Guided Sessions

- **Music-Assisted Relaxation:** These sessions use calming music to help you relax and let go of stress. They often include instructions for deep breathing and progressive muscle relaxation.
- **Sound Bath Meditations:** Sound baths involve listening to resonant sounds from instruments like singing bowls, gongs, and chimes. The vibrations from these sounds can induce deep relaxation and a meditative state.
- **Binaural Beats Meditation:** Guided meditations that incorporate binaural beats can help entrain your brain to desired states, such as relaxation or focus. These sessions typically involve listening to headphones for the full effect.

Finding Resources

There are numerous resources available online for guided meditation and relaxation sessions. Apps like Calm, Headspace, and Insight Timer offer a wide range of guided sessions with different types of music and sounds. YouTube and various meditation websites also provide free resources.

Everyone is unique. You'll have to experiment a bit to find the best music genres and types that help soothe your anxiety the most. To help you find the best resources for what you need, we can recommend a typical search online.

For example, a search for "music to soothe my anxiety" returned these results in the image below.

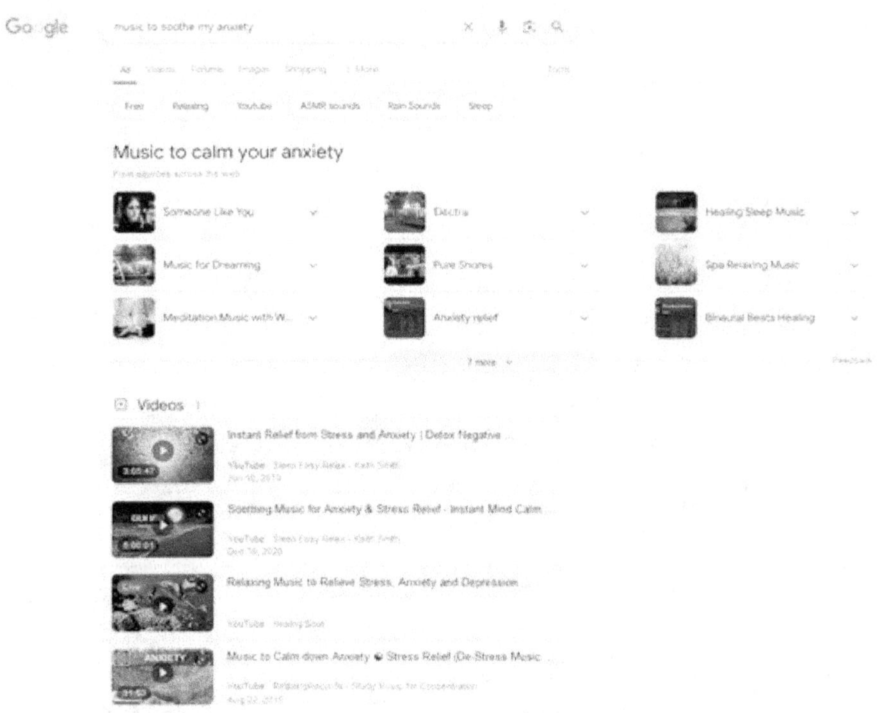

Search results for music to soothe my anxiety

And you can broaden your search or narrow it depending on the type(s) of music that appeal to you. For example, if you add the term "jazz" to your search the results below are returned by Google search engines.

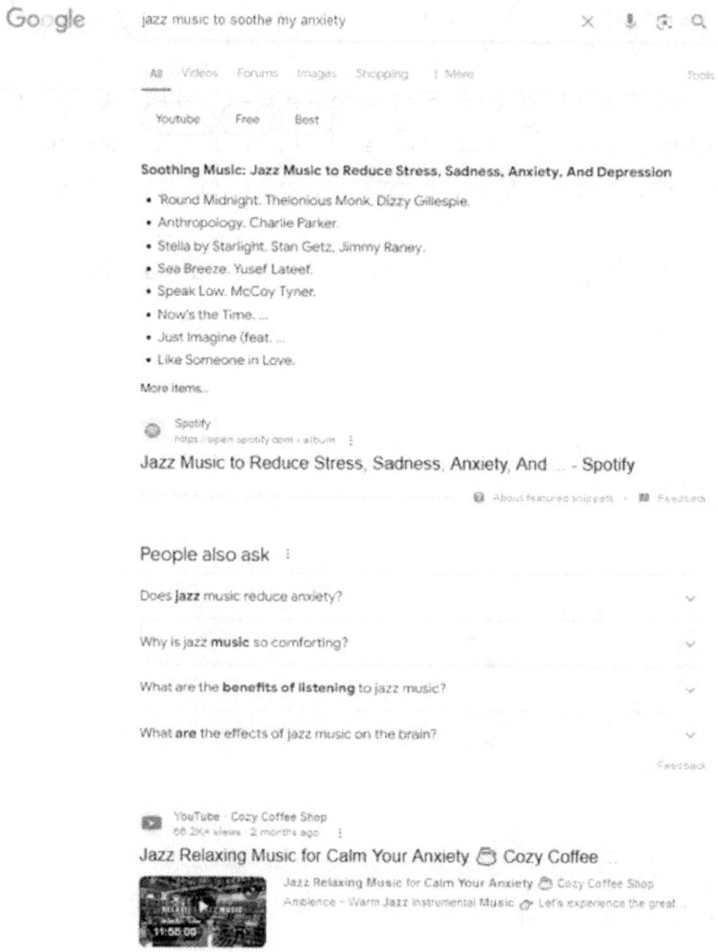

Personally I happen to like Thelonius Monk, Dizzy Gillespie, Stan Getz and a few of the others at the top of these results. But that's what works for me.

For you, online search and exploration of all the sources available to you will get you where you need to be. Don't be afraid to experiment and even try new types of music to get the maximum benefits.

Sound Therapy Techniques

Sound therapy involves using specific sounds and frequencies to promote healing and relaxation. Here are some popular techniques you can try:

Singing Bowls

Singing bowls, often made of metal or crystal, produce rich, harmonic sounds when struck or played with a mallet. The vibrations from the bowls can create a calming atmosphere and help reduce stress.

Tuning Forks

Tuning forks are tools that produce a specific pitch when struck. They are used in sound therapy to balance the body's energy and promote relaxation. Tuning fork therapy can be self-administered or performed by a trained practitioner.

White Noise and Nature Sounds

Listening to white noise or nature sounds, such as rain, ocean waves, or forest sounds, can be very soothing. These sounds can mask distracting noises and create a peaceful environment, which is especially helpful for sleep and relaxation.

Using Music and Sound in Therapy

Music and sound can be powerful adjuncts to traditional therapy. Here are some ways they can be integrated:

Music Therapy Sessions

In music therapy, a trained therapist uses music to address emotional, cognitive, and social needs. Sessions might include listening to music, playing instruments, singing, or songwriting. Music therapy can help individuals express emotions, develop coping skills, and improve mental health.

EMDR with Bilateral Sounds

Eye Movement Desensitization and Reprocessing (EMDR) is a therapy technique that uses bilateral stimulation, such as alternating sounds in each ear, to help process traumatic memories. This method can reduce the emotional impact of traumatic experiences and alleviate anxiety.

DIY Sound Therapy Tools

Creating a dedicated space for sound therapy at home can enhance your practice. Here are some tools and tips:

Essential Tools

- **Quality Headphones:** Invest in a good pair of headphones for listening to binaural beats or guided sessions.
- **Singing Bowls and Tuning Forks:** These can be purchased online or at specialty stores. Practice using them to find the sounds that resonate best with you.
- **White Noise Machine:** A white noise machine can provide consistent background noise to aid relaxation and sleep.

Creating a Calming Environment

- **Quiet Space:** Find a quiet area in your home where you can practice sound therapy without interruptions.
- **Comfortable Seating:** Use a comfortable chair or cushion for meditation and relaxation sessions.
- **Aromatherapy:** Enhance your environment with calming scents like lavender or chamomile using essential oils or candles.

Conclusion

By integrating music and sound into your daily routines, creating personalized playlists, engaging in guided meditation, and exploring sound therapy techniques, you can effectively manage anxiety and stress. These practical applications provide accessible, enjoyable, and powerful ways to enhance your well-being. Whether you use them alone or in conjunction with traditional treatments, the healing power of music and sound can become an invaluable part of your journey toward better mental health.

5

Special Techniques and Tools

In this chapter, we will delve into special techniques and tools that harness the power of music and sound to lower anxiety and stress. We will cover how to use various methods, including binaural beats, bilateral sound, and other sound therapy tools, to enhance your mental and emotional well-being. By the end of this chapter, you will have a clear understanding of how to implement these techniques effectively in your daily life.

Binaural Beats

Binaural beats are an auditory phenomenon created by playing two slightly different frequencies in each ear. The brain perceives a third tone that is the mathematical difference between the two, which can help entrain the brain to specific states.

How to Use Binaural Beats

1. **Choose the Right Frequency:** Identify the brainwave state you wish to target:

- **Delta (1-4 Hz):** Deep sleep and relaxation
- **Theta (4-8 Hz):** Meditation, creativity, and deep relaxation

- **Alpha (8-12 Hz):** Relaxed alertness and stress reduction
- **Beta (12-30 Hz):** Active thinking and focus

1. **Use Headphones:** Binaural beats require the use of stereo headphones to ensure each ear receives a different frequency.
2. **Find a Quiet Space:** Choose a quiet, comfortable environment where you can relax without interruptions.
3. **Listen for 15-30 Minutes:** Spend at least 15-30 minutes listening to binaural beats. You can find binaural beat tracks on streaming platforms, specialized apps, or YouTube.
4. **Incorporate into Daily Routine:** Use binaural beats during meditation, before sleep, or while working to achieve the desired state of mind.

Practical Tips

- **Consistency:** Regular listening can enhance the effectiveness of binaural beats.
- **Comfortable Volume:** Keep the volume at a comfortable level to avoid ear strain.
- **Mindfulness Practice:** Combine binaural beats with mindfulness practices for enhanced benefits.

One of the best sources we've found for binaural beats comes from Helios Records (https://linktr.ee/heliosrecords). They've categorize hundreds of beats into various categories – concentration, relaxing, meditation, etc. as in the image below.

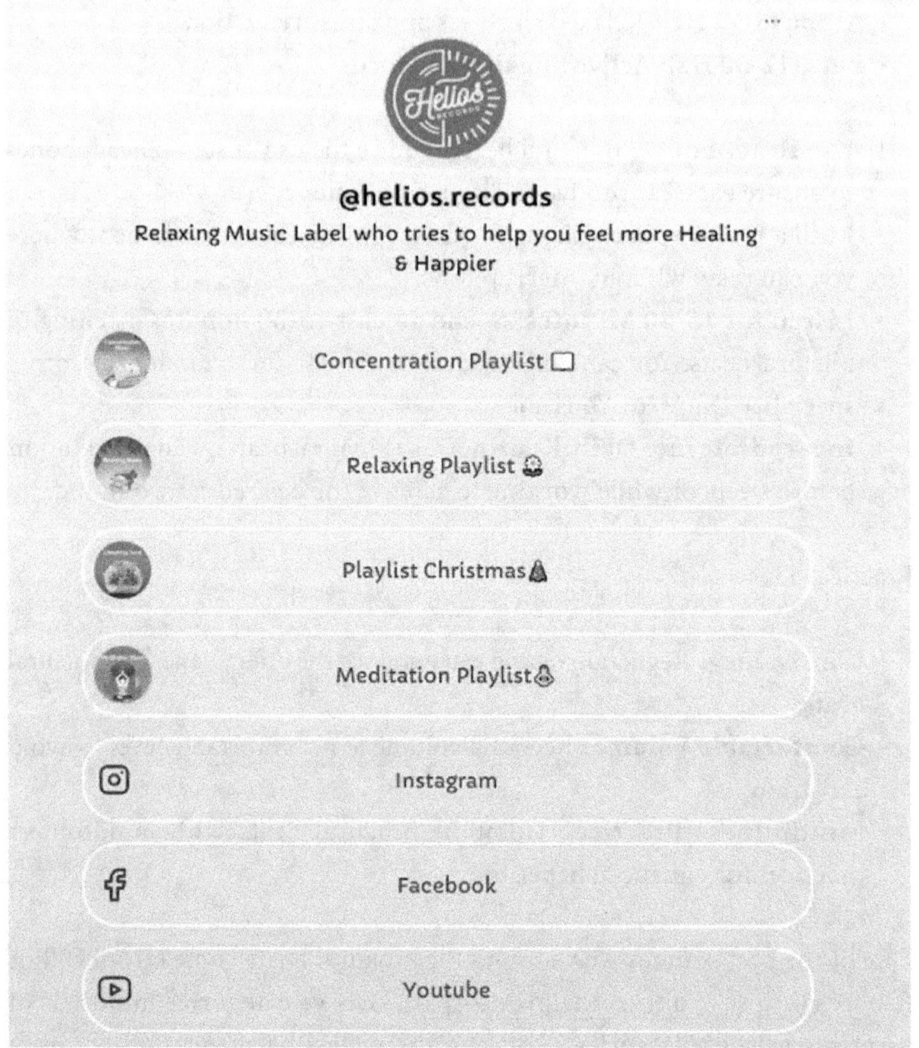

When you click on one of the categories you'll be able to see the selection under each group. For example, the listings under "Concentration" include 100 different tracks. And you can listen on the website or use their connection on Spotify for the full-length versions.

And as you are used to doing, if you simply search for a term like "binaural beats concentration" you'll get results like the image below from your regular search engine.

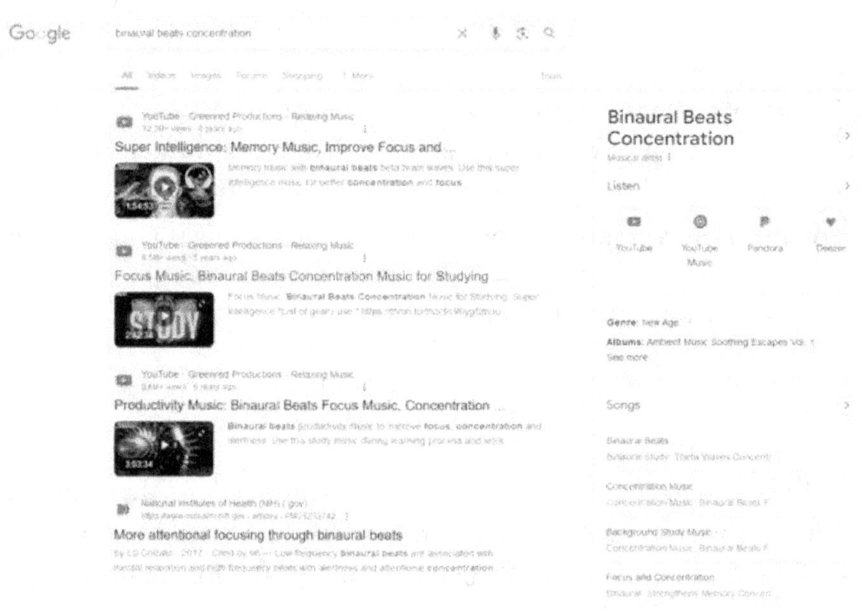

There are many resources you can find to access the binaural beats music you need to soothe your anxiety and lower your stress levels.

Bilateral Sound

Bilateral sound involves alternating audio stimulation between the left and right ears, often used in therapies such as Eye Movement Desensitization and Reprocessing (EMDR).

How to Use Bilateral Sound

1. **Choose Bilateral Sound Tracks:** Look for tracks specifically designed for bilateral stimulation. These are available on music streaming services, specialized therapy apps, and YouTube.
2. **Use Headphones:** Like binaural beats, bilateral sound requires stereo headphones to alternate sounds effectively between ears.
3. **Set a Relaxing Environment:** Find a quiet and comfortable place to sit or lie down.
4. **Listen for 10-20 Minutes:** Start with short sessions and gradually increase the duration as you become more comfortable with the technique.
5. **Focus on the Sensation:** Pay attention to the shifting sounds between your ears. This can help engage both hemispheres of the brain and promote relaxation.

Practical Tips

- **Guided Sessions:** Use guided bilateral sound sessions that combine verbal instructions with the sound for a more structured experience.
- **Therapeutic Use:** Consider using bilateral sound during self-reflection or journaling to help process emotions and reduce anxiety.

As with other types of music you can use yourself, a simple search for "bilateral beats" returns many options and details, as in the image below.

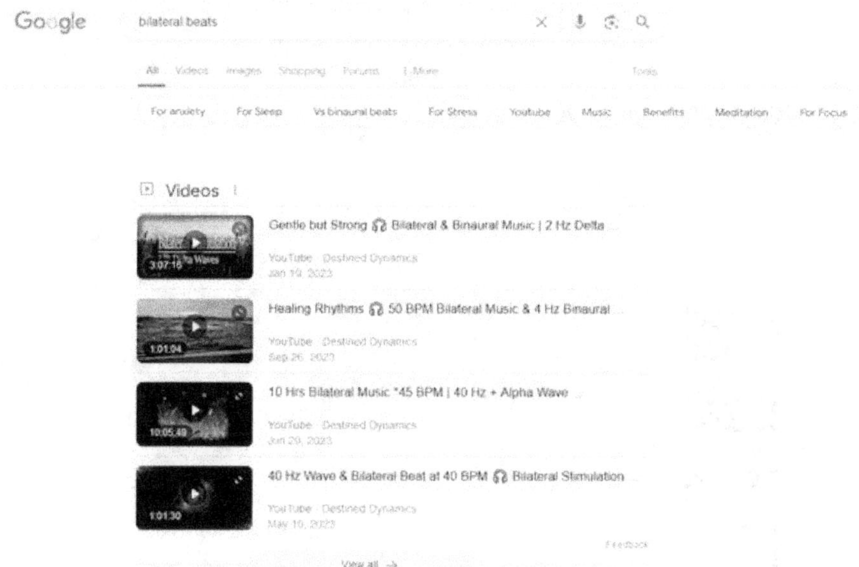

Note at the top of the search results you can find listings of bilateral beats "For anxiety" as well as other categories – sleep, stress, meditation, focus, etc.

Destined Dynamics in particular has a good selection of choices of bilateral music. See the image below for search results.

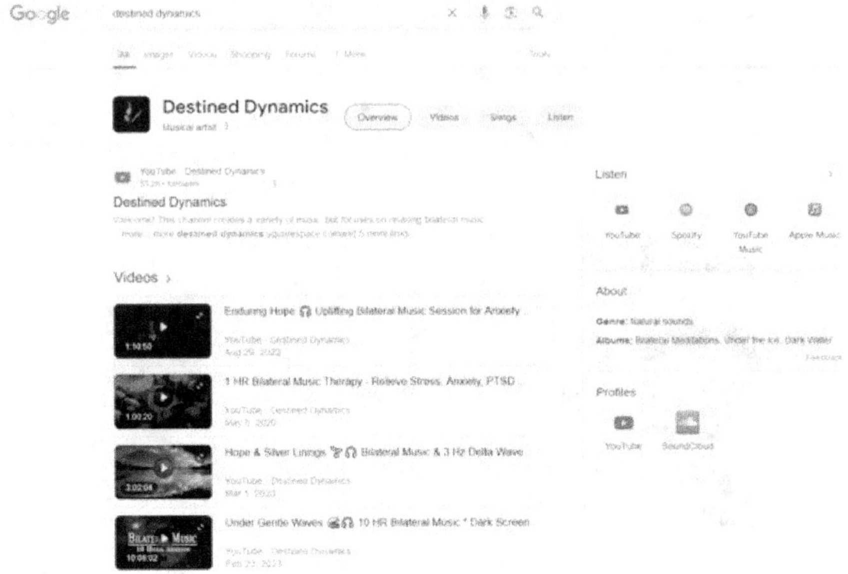

As with other types of sounds and music that you yourself can take advantage of I encourage you to experiment, try a few different things and go with what works best for you.

Sound Baths and Singing Bowls

Sound baths involve immersing yourself in the sounds of singing bowls, gongs, and other resonant instruments. These vibrations can induce deep relaxation and meditative states. Tibetan temple bells were one of my first experiences with sound bathing. I can highly recommend use of bowls and bells for the immersive method. Your brain will thank you.

How to Participate in a Sound Bath

1. **Find a Session:** Look for local sound bath events, or use online resources to find virtual sessions.
2. **Create a Comfortable Space:** If participating at home, set up a comfortable area with a mat, blanket, and pillows.

3. **Relax and Listen:** Lie down, close your eyes, and let the sounds wash over you. Focus on the vibrations and how they make your body feel.
4. **Duration:** Sessions typically last between 30 minutes to an hour.

How to Use Singing Bowls

1. **Choose a Bowl:** Select a singing bowl that resonates with you. Metal bowls have a variety of tones, while crystal bowls produce pure, clear sounds.
2. **Hold the Bowl:** Place the bowl on the palm of your hand or on a cushion.
3. **Strike and Play:** Gently strike the bowl with a mallet to produce a tone. To create a continuous sound, run the mallet around the rim of the bowl.
4. **Focus on the Sound:** Close your eyes and focus on the sound and vibrations, allowing yourself to relax deeply.

Practical Tips

- **Regular Practice:** Incorporate sound baths or singing bowls into your weekly routine for consistent benefits.
- **Mindful Listening:** Practice mindful listening during sound baths, paying attention to the changes in sound and how they affect your mind and body.

Tuning Forks

Tuning forks are used in sound therapy to produce specific frequencies that can balance the body's energy and promote relaxation.
How to Use Tuning Forks

1. **Choose the Right Fork:** Different tuning forks produce different frequencies. Some common ones include:

- **128 Hz:** For grounding and relaxation

- **136.1 Hz (Om):** For meditation and harmony
- **528 Hz:** For transformation and DNA repair

1. **Strike the Fork:** Gently strike the tuning fork against a rubber mallet or a surface to produce a tone.
2. **Apply Near the Body:** Hold the vibrating fork near your ears or place the stem on different parts of your body (e.g., shoulders, chest) to feel the vibrations.
3. **Listen and Feel:** Close your eyes and focus on the sound and sensations, allowing the vibrations to bring a sense of calm and balance.

Practical Tips

- **Deep Breathing:** Combine tuning fork therapy with deep breathing exercises for enhanced relaxation.
- **Regular Sessions:** Use tuning forks regularly to maintain a balanced and relaxed state.

A trip to the music store to look for different tuning forks can be a great adventure. Or you can purchase them online as well.

White Noise and Nature Sounds

White noise and nature sounds can create a calming background that helps mask distracting noises and promote relaxation.

How to Use White Noise and Nature Sounds

1. **Select Your Sound:** Choose from a variety of sounds, such as white noise, rain, ocean waves, or forest sounds. Many apps and online platforms offer these sounds.
2. **Set Up a Player:** Use a white noise machine, smartphone app, or online service to play the sounds.

3. **Create a Relaxing Environment:** Play the sounds in your bedroom, office, or any space where you need to reduce stress and enhance focus.
4. **Adjust Volume:** Set the volume to a comfortable level that effectively masks unwanted noises without being too loud.

Practical Tips

- **Sleep Aid:** Use white noise or nature sounds at bedtime to improve sleep quality and duration.
- **Focus and Productivity:** Play background sounds while working or studying to enhance concentration.

Conclusion

By incorporating these special techniques and tools into your routine, you can harness the power of music and sound to effectively lower anxiety and stress. Whether you choose binaural beats, bilateral sound, sound baths, tuning forks, or white noise, each method offers unique benefits that can enhance your mental and emotional well-being. Experiment with different techniques to find what works best for you, and integrate these practices into your daily life for lasting positive effects. And listening for 15-30 minutes per day can make a huge difference with consistent practice.

6

Expanding Your Practice

As you become more comfortable with using music and sound to manage anxiety and stress, you may want to expand and deepen your practice independently. This chapter will explore ways to take your sound therapy practice to the next level, focusing on techniques you can use on your own. From integrating other holistic practices to discovering new tools and technologies, you will learn how to enhance your personal journey toward mental and emotional well-being.

Integrating Other Holistic Practices

Combining sound therapy with other holistic practices can amplify its benefits and create a more comprehensive approach to managing anxiety and stress.

Yoga and Sound

Yoga and sound therapy can enhance each other, promoting relaxation and mindfulness.

1. **Sound-Infused Yoga at Home:** Incorporate calming music or nature sounds into your yoga practice. Create a playlist of soothing tracks to

32

play during your sessions.

2. **Use Singing Bowls:** During savasana (final relaxation pose), play a singing bowl to deepen relaxation. Strike the bowl gently and let the sound resonate as you focus on your breath.

3. **Yoga Nidra with Music:** Practice Yoga Nidra, a guided meditation that promotes deep relaxation, with a background of soft, ambient music.

Meditation and Mindfulness

Sound can be a powerful aid in meditation and mindfulness practices.

1. **Guided Sound Meditations:** Use guided meditations that incorporate soothing sounds, such as Tibetan singing bowls or ambient music. Apps like Calm, Insight Timer, and Headspace offer many options.

2. **Background Sounds for Silent Meditation:** Play gentle background sounds, such as nature sounds or white noise, during silent meditation sessions to create a calming atmosphere.

3. **Mindful Listening:** Practice mindful listening by focusing on a specific sound, like a singing bowl or a piece of music, and observing how it makes you feel without judgment.

Aromatherapy

Combining aromatherapy with sound therapy creates a multi-sensory experience that enhances relaxation.

1. **Essential Oils and Diffusers:** Use essential oils like lavender, chamomile, or eucalyptus in a diffuser during your sound therapy sessions. The combination of soothing sounds and calming scents can deepen relaxation.

2. **Aromatherapy Products:** Use aromatherapy candles, incense, or scented eye pillows during meditation or sound therapy practices to create a relaxing environment.

Exploring New Tools and Technologies

Staying informed about new tools and technologies can help you enhance and expand your sound therapy practice.

Apps and Software

Many apps and software programs are designed to support sound therapy and meditation practices.

1. **Meditation Apps:** Use apps like Calm, Headspace, and Insight Timer, which offer a variety of guided meditations, soundscapes, and music for relaxation.
2. **Sound Therapy Apps:** Explore apps like Brain.fm and MyNoise, which provide customized soundscapes and binaural beats designed to promote relaxation, focus, and sleep.
3. **White Noise and Nature Sound Apps:** Apps like Relax Melodies and Rain Rain provide a wide range of white noise and nature sounds that can help you relax and concentrate.

New Instruments and Devices

Explore new sound therapy instruments and devices as they become available.

1. **Innovative Sound Tools:** Look for new instruments, such as electronic sound healing devices or innovative tuning fork sets, to add to your practice.
2. **Wearable Technology:** Consider wearable devices designed to promote relaxation through sound and vibration, such as smart headphones or haptic feedback wearables.

DIY Sound Therapy Techniques

Creating your own sound therapy sessions at home can be both empowering and effective. Here are some DIY techniques you can use to deepen your practice.

Creating Soundscapes

1. **Mix Your Own Soundscapes:** Use sound mixing software or apps to create custom soundscapes that combine different elements like ambient music, nature sounds, and binaural beats.
2. **Experiment with Layers:** Layer different sounds to create a rich, immersive experience. For example, combine the sound of rain with soft piano music and distant thunder.

Using Singing Bowls

1. **Daily Practice:** Integrate singing bowls into your daily routine. Spend a few minutes each day striking the bowl and focusing on the sound and its vibrations.
2. **Sound Meditation:** Use singing bowls during meditation sessions. Strike the bowl at the beginning and end of your meditation to mark the start and finish.

Tuning Fork Therapy

1. **Self-Application:** Use tuning forks on yourself by striking the fork and placing it near your ears or on different parts of your body. Focus on the vibrations and how they affect you.
2. **Combining with Breathing Exercises:** Combine tuning fork therapy with deep breathing exercises to enhance relaxation and balance.

Creating a Calming Environment

1. **Quiet Space:** Designate a quiet area in your home where you can practice sound therapy without interruptions. Use comfortable seating and calming decor.
2. **Ambient Lighting:** Use soft, ambient lighting such as candles or salt lamps to create a relaxing atmosphere.
3. **Personal Altar:** Create a personal altar or sacred space with objects that bring you peace, such as crystals, essential oils, and meaningful symbols.

Staying Informed: Research and Developments

Keeping up with the latest research and developments in sound therapy can help you stay informed and inspired.

Scientific Journals and Publications

Read scientific journals and publications that focus on music therapy, sound healing, and related fields.

1. **Journal of Music Therapy:** This peer-reviewed journal publishes research articles on all aspects of music therapy.
2. **Frontiers in Psychology:** This open-access journal often features articles on the psychological effects of music and sound.

Books and Articles

Read books and articles by experts in the field to gain deeper insights and knowledge.

1. **Books:** Look for books on sound healing, music therapy, and holistic health written by reputable authors.
2. **Online Articles:** Many websites and blogs offer articles on the latest trends and research in sound therapy.

Online Courses and Webinars

Participate in online courses and webinars to continue learning and expanding your knowledge.

1. **Webinars by Experts:** Attend webinars hosted by experts in sound therapy and music therapy. These sessions often cover advanced techniques and the latest research.
2. **Online Courses:** Enroll in online courses that provide structured learning and certification in sound therapy or music therapy.

Conclusion

Expanding your practice with music and sound independently involves integrating other holistic practices, exploring new tools and technologies, and staying informed about the latest research. By continuously learning and evolving your approach, you can deepen your understanding and effectiveness in using sound therapy to manage anxiety and stress. Embrace these opportunities to grow and enrich your practice, creating a more comprehensive and fulfilling path to mental and emotional well-being.

7

Personal Stories and Case Studies

Understanding the impact of music and sound therapy on real people can be both inspiring and insightful. In this chapter, we delve into personal stories and case studies that illustrate the profound effects sound therapy can have on managing anxiety and stress. These examples provide concrete evidence of how sound therapy works in different contexts and for various individuals.

Case Study 1: Sarah's Journey with Sound Baths

Background

Sarah, a 35-year-old marketing executive, struggled with severe anxiety and chronic stress due to her high-pressure job. She often experienced panic attacks and found it difficult to relax, even outside of work hours. Traditional methods of managing anxiety, such as medication and cognitive-behavioral therapy, provided some relief but did not fully address her symptoms.

Discovery of Sound Baths

Sarah was introduced to sound baths through a friend who invited her to a local sound healing event. Skeptical but hopeful, she attended her first session, where she was enveloped in the harmonious sounds of gongs, crystal singing bowls, and chimes.

The Experience

During the sound bath, Sarah lay on a mat with her eyes closed, surrounded by soothing sounds. The session lasted for an hour, during which she felt a deep sense of relaxation and peace that she had not experienced in years. The vibrations from the instruments seemed to penetrate her body, calming her mind and easing her tension. Every one of us is unique and Sarah's experience with her first sound bath event may not be the same as yours. But be encouraged and keep experimenting to find what works best for you.

Integration into Daily Life

Encouraged by the profound relaxation she felt, Sarah began attending weekly sound baths. She also invested in a set of crystal singing bowls to use at home. Incorporating sound baths into her routine significantly reduced her anxiety levels. She found that the regular exposure to the calming sounds helped her to manage stress more effectively, preventing panic attacks and improving her overall quality of life.

Outcome

After six months of regular sound baths, Sarah reported a dramatic decrease in her anxiety symptoms. Her panic attacks became rare, and she developed a healthier relationship with her work. Sarah's experience underscores the potential of sound baths to provide relief for those struggling with severe anxiety.

Case Study 2: John's Success with Binaural Beats

Background

John, a 28-year-old software developer, experienced high levels of stress due to long working hours and the demanding nature of his job. He often found it difficult to switch off his mind, leading to insomnia and increased anxiety. Despite trying various relaxation techniques, he struggled to find a method that effectively helped him to unwind.

Introduction to Binaural Beats

John came across binaural beats while browsing for stress-relief techniques online. Intrigued by the scientific basis behind them, he decided to give it a try. He started with a free app that offered binaural beat tracks designed to promote relaxation and sleep.

The Process

John began incorporating binaural beats into his nightly routine. He would listen to alpha and theta wave binaural beats for 30 minutes before going to bed. Using stereo headphones, he allowed the gentle pulsations to ease his mind into a relaxed state.

Changes and Benefits

Within a week, John noticed a significant improvement in his ability to fall asleep and stay asleep. The binaural beats helped to quiet his racing thoughts and induced a sense of calm that he had not experienced with other methods. Encouraged by these results, he started using binaural beats during work breaks to manage stress and maintain focus.

Outcome

Over time, John's anxiety levels decreased, and he reported feeling more balanced and less overwhelmed by his job. The binaural beats became an essential part of his stress-management toolkit, demonstrating how this simple yet powerful technique can provide significant relief for those dealing with chronic stress and anxiety.

Case Study 3: Emily's Transformation with Bilateral Sound

Background

Emily, a 42-year-old teacher, suffered from post-traumatic stress disorder (PTSD) due to a traumatic event she experienced several years ago. Despite undergoing therapy, she continued to struggle with anxiety, flashbacks, and insomnia. Emily was looking for an alternative method to supplement her ongoing treatment.

Introduction to Bilateral Sound

Emily's therapist recommended bilateral sound as part of her treatment plan. Bilateral sound involves alternating audio stimulation between the left and right ears, which can help process traumatic memories and reduce anxiety. Emily began using an app that provided bilateral sound tracks specifically designed for trauma therapy.

The Process

Emily used the bilateral sound tracks during her daily meditation sessions. She would find a quiet space, put on her headphones, and listen to the alternating sounds for 20 minutes. The sounds helped her to focus and facilitated a sense of balance and calm.

Impact and Progress

After a few weeks of regular use, Emily noticed a reduction in the intensity and frequency of her flashbacks. The bilateral sound sessions helped her to process her traumatic memories more effectively, reducing her overall anxiety levels. She also experienced improvements in her sleep quality, as the bilateral sounds helped her to relax before bedtime.

Outcome

Over several months, Emily experienced significant improvements in her mental health. The combination of bilateral sound therapy and traditional therapy provided a comprehensive approach to managing her PTSD. Emily's case highlights the potential of bilateral sound to aid in the treatment of trauma-related anxiety, offering a powerful tool for those seeking alternative therapies.

Conclusion

These case studies illustrate the transformative power of sound therapy in managing anxiety and stress. From Sarah's relief through sound baths to John's success with binaural beats and Emily's transformation with bilateral sound, these stories provide concrete examples of how different sound therapy techniques can be tailored to individual needs. By exploring these personal stories, readers can gain inspiration and insight into how they might incorporate sound therapy into their own lives, finding effective ways to manage anxiety and enhance their overall well-being. And please note that for some of us combining sound and music complements traditional therapy as in Emily's case. Always seek professional help if you think you need it.

8

Conclusion

As we reach the conclusion of our exploration into the world of music and sounds as a therapeutic tool for anxiety and stress relief, it's clear that the power of these auditory elements extends far beyond simple entertainment. Through the detailed discussions in this book, we've uncovered not just the scientific mechanisms that underpin sound therapy, but also practical ways to integrate this knowledge into everyday life, harnessing sound's profound ability to heal and soothe the human mind and spirit.

Summarizing Key Insights

We began by understanding the fundamental relationship between sound and human physiology, learning how certain frequencies and rhythms can interact directly with our brainwaves to induce states of relaxation and peace. The science of music and sound presented in Chapter 2 illuminated the biological and psychological effects that contribute to its efficacy as a form of therapy.

From there, we explored practical applications in Chapter 3, detailing how different environments and personal practices can be enriched with sound to reduce anxiety. Techniques such as listening to specific types of music, creating personal playlists, engaging with sound baths, and utilizing the therapeutic effects of nature's own soundscape were discussed, providing a toolkit for anyone to use.

In Chapter 4, we dove deeper into specialized techniques and tools, including binaural beats and bilateral sound, which offer more targeted approaches for those who might need additional support in managing their anxiety. The ability to use these tools effectively at home, as well as in clinical or therapeutic settings, opens up numerous possibilities for individualized care.

Chapter 5 brought the real-life impact of these theories into light, with personal stories and case studies that showcased the transformative power of sound on individuals' lives. These stories not only served as testimonials to the effectiveness of sound therapy but also provided inspiration and hope to those seeking relief from their own struggles with anxiety.

Emphasizing Self-Empowerment

Chapter 6 reinforced the empowering aspect of sound therapy, emphasizing how individuals can take control of their mental health through self-guided practices. By equipping ourselves with knowledge and tools to manage anxiety independently, sound therapy encourages a proactive approach to mental health care, promoting resilience and self-sufficiency.

Moving Forward

As readers, you are now armed with a deeper understanding of how sound can be a powerful ally against anxiety and stress. The rhythmic tapping of rain, the complex harmonies of a symphony, or the simple melody of a lullaby all have the potential for healing within the sounds that surround us daily.

I encourage you to experiment with the concepts and techniques discussed in this book. Begin by integrating small changes in your listening environment, and observe the effects on your mood and anxiety levels. Consider sound therapy not just as a method for crisis management, but as a daily practice for maintaining mental health and well-being.

A Lasting Echo

Let the lessons and stories within these pages resonate like a harmonious melody that lingers long after the music stops. May this book serve not only as a guide but as a continual source of comfort and inspiration, helping you to navigate life's challenges with a little more harmony and a lot less anxiety. Through sound, you hold the power to orchestrate a more serene and calmer existence.

9

Resources

The journey toward using music and sound as therapeutic tools doesn't end with the last chapter of this book. To further assist you in implementing sound therapy into your daily life and deepening your understanding of its principles and techniques, the following resources and tools are provided. Here, you will find a curated list of apps, websites, playlists, books, and professional associations that can offer guidance, practical tools, and community support.

A. Recommended Listening

1. Therapeutic Playlists

- Spotify: Collections of playlists designed for relaxation, sleep, concentration, and stress relief.
- Apple Music: Curated playlists featuring calming music, nature sounds, and instrumental tracks.

1. Binaural Beats and Bilateral Sounds

- YouTube: Channels dedicated to binaural beats for different states like relaxation, meditation, and sleep.

- Insight Timer: Free app with a wide range of binaural tracks and guided meditations.

B. Sound Therapy Apps

1. **Calm**: Offers guided meditations, sleep stories, and a variety of nature sounds to help reduce anxiety and improve the quality of sleep.
2. **Headspace**: Provides themed sessions on everything from stress and sleep to focus and anxiety, including sound-based meditations.
3. **MyNoise**: A unique app that allows users to customize sounds across a wide spectrum, focusing on soundscapes that promote concentration and relaxation.
4. **Atmosphere**: An app designed to create immersive environments using a mix of natural and synthetic sounds, ideal for relaxation and meditation.

C. Books and Literature

1. **"The Power of Music: Pioneering Discoveries in the New Science of Song" by Elena Mannes** - Explores how music affects different stages of human life and overall well-being.
2. **"This Is Your Brain on Music: The Science of a Human Obsession" by Daniel J. Levitin** - Discusses how the brain interprets music and its effect on emotions and cognition.
3. **"Healing at the Speed of Sound: How What We Hear Transforms Our Brains and Our Lives" by Don Campbell and Alex Doman** - Provides insight into how sound and music can be used to enhance quality of life in various aspects, from stress reduction to increased efficiency.

D. Professional Organizations

1. **The American Music Therapy Association (AMTA)**: Provides resources, support, and a directory of certified music therapists who specialize in using music to help individuals improve their health and well-being.
2. **The Sound Healers Association**: Dedicated to the research and education of sound healing, offering workshops, seminars, and conferences.

E. Online Courses and Workshops

1. **Udemy**: Offers various courses on sound therapy, binaural beats, and how to use sound for relaxation and stress management.
2. **The Sound Healing Academy**: Provides online courses and certifications in sound therapy, teaching therapeutic sound techniques and their application.

F. DIY Tools for Sound Therapy

- **Instructions for DIY Sound Instruments**: Guides on creating your own sound therapy tools, such as rain sticks, simple drums, or chimes.
- **Guides on Recording Natural Sounds**: Tips for capturing high-quality audio recordings of nature sounds, which can be used for personal meditation and relaxation.

This appendix is intended to be a living document, continually updated with the latest resources and findings in the field of sound therapy. Whether you are a beginner looking to explore the basics or an experienced practitioner seeking to deepen your practice, these resources offer valuable support as you incorporate the healing power of sound into your life.

About the Author

Mr. Allman earned a Ph.D. in counseling and has spent thousands of hours talking with people and groups about their anxiety and stress. With his research and analytics background, he likes to use the latest science and technology to solve big problems in big markets. He's fond of horses, motorcycles and American muscle cars, in that order. Most often, you can find Dale outdoors.

You can connect with me on:
- https://www.creativedatanetworks.com
- https://www.twitter.com/dna_books
- https://www.facebook.com/DaleAllmanBooks
- https://www.instagram.com/dnabooksoffical

Subscribe to my newsletter:
- https://www.trueanxietyrelief.com